HOW? WHO? WHAT? WHEN? WHERE? WHY?

ABOUT
EARTH AND SKY

PUBLISHER	Joseph R. DeVarennes	
PUBLICATION DIRECTOR	Kenneth H. Pearson	
ADVISORS	Roger Aubin	
	Robert Furlonger	
EDITORIAL SUPERVISOR	Jocelyn Smyth	
PRODUCTION MANAGER	Ernest Homewood	
PRODUCTION ASSISTANTS	Martine Gingras	Kathy Kishimoto
	Catherine Gordon	Peter Thomlison
CONTRIBUTORS	Alison Dickie	Nancy Prasad
	Bill Ivy	Lois Rock
	Jacqueline Kendel	Merebeth Switzer
	Anne Langdon	Dave Taylor
	Sheila Macdonald	Alison Tharen
	Susan Marshall	Donna Thomson
	Pamela Martin	Pam Young
	Colin McCance	
SENIOR EDITOR	Robin Rivers	
EDITORS	Brian Cross	Ann Martin
	Anne Louise Mahoney	Mayta Tannenbaum
PUBLICATION ADMINISTRATOR	Anna Good	
ART AND DESIGN	Richard Comely	Ronald Migliore
	George Elliott	Sue Wilkinson
	Greg Elliott	

Canadian Cataloguing in Publication Data

Questions kids ask about earth and sky

(Questions kids ask ; 3)
ISBN 0-7172-2390-6

1. Earth—Miscellanea—Juvenile literature. 2. Weather—Miscellanea—
Juvenile literature.   3. Sky—Miscellanea—Juvenile literature.
4. Children's questions and answers.   I. Comely, Richard.
II. Wilkinson, Sue.   III. Elliott, Greg.   IV. Series.

QE29.Q48 1988   j550   C88-093576-6

Questions Kids Ask...about EARTH AND SKY

continued

Why is sea water so salty?

Sea water tastes salty because of the minerals washed into it from the land. As rivers flow over the land they pick up, or dissolve, some minerals and carry them to the ocean. The minerals that are picked up most easily are sodium and chloride. Together, they make the salt we use to season our food.

Sea water is constantly evaporating, but the minerals in it are left behind. Rivers have been carrying salt into the sea for millions of years. No wonder it tastes so salty!

How much does the earth weigh?

The earth is a huge ball of hot rock and metal surrounded by a thin rocky crust covered with water and soil. How much do you think all of this would weigh if you could somehow put it on a scale?

According to scientists, the earth weighs 6600 BILLION, BILLION tons! That's 6 000 000 000 000 000 000 000 kilograms (13 200 000 000 000 000 000 000 pounds)!

5

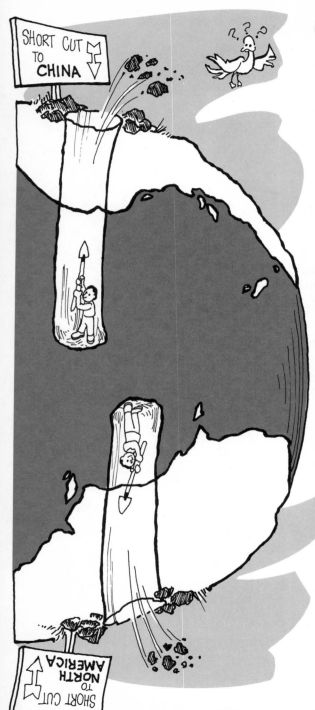

SHORT CUT TO CHINA

SHORT CUT TO NORTH AMERICA

Can you dig to China?

If you carried a shovel into your backyard and started to dig, would you eventually end up in China? Not even close!

China is on the opposite side of the world from us, so it might seem if you dug straight down you would end up there. However, it is not possible to dig right through the earth.

And it would be a lot of hard, hot work trying to get there. Beneath its crust of soil and dirt the earth is a huge ball of hot rock and metal. A thick layer of solid rock goes down about 2900 kilometres (1800 miles). Beneath that, there's about 2300 kilometres (1400 miles) of melted iron and nickel. If you could get through all of that, you'd be nearly at the center of the earth. There you'd run into solid iron and nickel. And you'd better bring a fan—the temperature there can be as high as 5000 degrees celsius (9000° F)!

So if you want to go to China, hop on a plane or boat. You could dig forever, and still not get there!

How deep is the Grand Canyon?

One of the most incredible sights in the world is the Grand Canyon in northern Arizona. It looks like a huge mountain turned upside down.

The Grand Canyon is actually a gorge which has been cut out of the earth by the force of water from the Colorado River. It has taken millions of years for the water to dig a hole so deep.

The Grand Canyon is now over 450 kilometres (280 miles) long. In some spots it is 29 kilometres (18 miles) wide. At its deepest point the Grand Canyon is 2 kilometres (over one mile) deep. That's a long way down!

Every year thousands of people travel to Grand Canyon National Park to see this beautiful natural sight.

What are stalactites and stalagmites?

They are beautiful rock formations that look a little bit like huge, colorful icicles. They are found deep inside dark caverns. Stalactites hang down from the ceilings of caves, while stalagmites rise up from the floor.

Water and a mineral called calcite work together to slowly build these natural wonders. Water drips through the cracks in the roof of a cave and carries calcite with it. When the water dries up, the mineral is left. Sometimes, the two rocky icicles will join—one growing down from the ceiling and the other rising up from the floor to meet it! In this way they can form columns or stone curtains against the walls of caves.

They are usually found in limestone caves, but can also develop out of lava (hot rock flowing from a volcano), or ice.

Does it ever snow on the equator?

You probably know that the equator is an imaginary line running around the earth half-way between the North and South poles. You probably also know that it is HOT there—like summer all the time.

Does this mean it never snows at the equator? Not quite. There are a few places near the equator where it does snow. The higher you go above the sea, the cooler the air is. Mountains at the equator, if they are high enough, can have weather patterns like those in very cold places. One such mountain is Mount Kilimanjaro in Tanzania, which is 5964 metres (19 680 feet) high. It is just south of the equator and is snow-covered all year round.

Why is ice slippery?

Strange as it may seem, ice itself really isn't slippery. It is a thin film of water (which we usually can't see) on top of ice that makes us slip.

When we step onto a patch of ice, it may *look* dry, but the pressure and movement of our feet cause some of the ice on the surface to melt. Although this action produces only a very thin layer of water, it is enough to allow us to slip on a frozen sidewalk.

Where are the coldest and hottest places on earth?

The coldest temperature ever recorded on earth was –88° C (–126° F) in Antarctica. Even in the most severe winter weather, temperatures in North America don't often go much below –40° C (–40° F).

As for the warmest temperature, the record goes to the Sahara Desert. Here the thermometer has hit a scorching 58° C (136° F). For comparison's sake, a heat wave in the southern United States would be considered deadly if it hit 48° C (120° F).

Is the tundra really treeless?

The tundra is one of the harshest places on earth. Located on both sides of the Arctic Circle, it is a land of bitter winds, little rainfall, long cold winters and short, barely warm summers. The tundra is often said to be treeless and it appears to be so. Indeed, if you are looking for a stately oak or maple, you will be disappointed. Instead you must look down. There *are* trees on the tundra, but few grow even as tall as a person. They stay low to the ground where they can be covered by snow and protected against the winds. They also grow very slowly.

Does a balloon go up forever in space?

Remember the balloon you got the last time you were at a circus? That's right, the one that floated in the air by itself! What would happen if you let it go? Would it make it to the moon?

No, it would come down eventually. Balloons that rise are filled with helium, the second lightest of all the gases on earth. It weighs less than the air around it, so helium rises— just as your beach ball does when you try to hold it down in the water.

The air closer to the ground is quite heavy, or dense, but farther away from the earth's surface it becomes thinner. A run-away balloon floats up and up . . . until it reaches a spot where the weight of the helium is equal to the weight of the air. And there it stops rising.

But sooner or later, the helium gas starts to leak out of the balloon and it sinks back down to earth. It might land in your own neighborhood, or it might drift great distances on the wind. Balloons have been known to drift over 1600 kilometres (1000 miles). That's not nearly as far as the moon, but it's pretty good for a balloon, don't you think?

DID YOU KNOW . . . the reason it is difficult to see through fog is because of the billions of tiny droplets of water suspended in the air. Each droplet scatters any light that shines into it and this makes it difficult for us to see.

Why are stars invisible during the day?

If you go outside on any clear night you will see millions of twinkling stars against the night sky, gleaming like sparkling jewels. Where do they go in the daytime?

The stars shine day and night, but we can see them only when the sky is dark and clear. During the day, the sun gives off so much light that the sky is brightened and you cannot see the rest of the stars, even though they are there. At night, when the sun's light is no longer shining directly down on us, the sky is darkened and once again we can see the brilliant twinkle of the stars.

Do clouds ever touch the ground?

They most certainly do. In fact, you've probably walked in a cloud before! A cloud that is on the ground is called fog.

Fog is formed when there is more moisture in the air than the air can hold. At this point, water droplets form around particles of dust, smoke and salt which are always in the air. Warm air can hold more moisture than cold, so when warm air full of moisture is cooled, the result is a fog.

A fog can form when warm moist air passes over a cold wet surface. It can also happen when cold air passes over a warm wet surface.

So the next time you are outside in a fog, think of it as walking through a cloud.

IT'S ELEMENTARY WATSON. FOG IS WATER DROPLETS IN THE AIR. WATSON? ...WATSON!

What is the Big Dipper?

The Big Dipper is a group of seven bright stars that form the shape of a dipper or ladle. It is part of a constellation—a group of stars that seem to make a picture of something. The constellation containing the Big Dipper is called *Ursa Major.*

There are 88 constellations now recognized and classified by astronomers. Many of them form pictures of a familiar object or animal. The constellation *Ursa Major,* for example, has the shape of a big bear. Astronomers, people who study stars and planets, group the stars into constellations in order to identify them more easily.

This has been done since very early times. A second-century astronomer, Ptolemy, named 48 constellations, most of which we still recognize today. European astronomers of the seventeenth and eighteenth centuries named the other 40.

Your local planetarium or astronomical society probably has star maps for your area. Why not get one and see how many constellations you can see on a clear night?

What is a falling star?

Some night when it is clear, take a look at the sky. If you are patient—and lucky—you may see a bright light streak in the sky. A falling star!

Of course real stars do not fall. What you saw was a meteor that hit the earth's atmosphere. A meteor is a piece of space junk; a bit of ice and rock left over from some unknown explosion in space.

When meteors hit the earth's atmosphere, friction causes them to heat up. To understand what friction is, rub your hands together. Feel the warmth? The friction between the speeding particle and the air is much greater. The particle gets so hot it glows and burns up. To us on earth it looks like a falling star.

Sometimes a larger piece of matter flashes through the sky without burning up completely. This is called a meteorite. Some huge meteorites have hit the earth and caused enormous craters. Fortunately most are the size of pebbles.

What causes thunder and lightning?

The flashes of light and booms of thunder during a storm can be awfully frightening. Scientists don't know exactly how lightning forms, but they do know part of the answer.

Have you ever crossed a carpet in stocking feet, then touched something and felt a tiny shock? The shock was caused by a buildup of electrical charge in your body, which you released by touching something. This is similar to what happens in a thundercloud.

Clouds are made of countless water droplets, and each one has a positive or negative electrical charge. In a thundercloud, the positively and negatively charged drops become separated from each other. Opposite charges are attracted to each other, but the air between the two areas prevents the charges from rushing together—until the charge becomes so great that a huge electric spark flashes across the gap. This spark is lightning.

When lightning flashes it heats the air along its path by many thousands of degrees. The heat causes the air to expand instantly and collide with the surrounding cooler air. This violent collision causes the booming sound of thunder.

We see the lightning before we hear the thunder because light travels faster than sound. Light travels at about 300 000 kilometres (186 000 miles) per second while sound travels only 330 metres (1100 feet) per second.

14

What causes avalanches?

An avalanche begins when a mass of snow piles up on a steep slope. A little push is all it needs to come rushing down, covering everything in its path. The push might come from the wind, earth tremors, thunder, gunfire, a branch falling or a person walking across the snow in the right place. Even a loud shout can start an avalanche, and mountain guides often demand silence when crossing dangerous spots.

Experts can often recognize the conditions that lead to an avalanche. To help prevent avalanches they use explosives to scatter the snow and prevent it from building up. Usually it works but not always.

What is a tornado?

A tornado is a wind tunnel that spins in a circle while moving across the ground. It looks like a funnel-shaped cloud. Because it spins so quickly—sometimes at speeds as great as 480 kilometres (300 miles) per hour—it pulls anything underneath it up into the air. Even things as large as trees or cars might be pulled off the ground, and buildings could be knocked over.

Tornadoes move along a path that is only several hundred metres (yards) wide. This is why it is possible for one house to be

destroyed by a tornado while the house next door is not even touched.

Each tornado only lasts a few minutes. But that's long enough to destroy a town that took hundreds of years to build.

DID YOU KNOW . . . tornadoes are most common in the United States, which has around 150 a year!

What is an asteroid?

Asteroids are actually tiny planets which revolve around the sun. Most of them travel in a belt between Mars and Jupiter. Scientists have spotted thousands of asteroids and studied many of them closely. Only one asteroid, named Vesta, is large enough and close enough to the earth to be seen without a telescope.

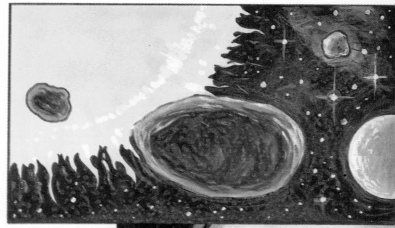

The largest known asteroid is called Ceres. It is about 770 kilometres (480 miles) across and was first discovered in 1801 by an Italian astronomer who thought he had discovered a new star.

Asteroids were once thought to be the remains of bigger planets that crashed into each other and broke apart. Now scientists believe that they were formed in the same way as the rest of the planets in the solar system, but never grew to be full-sized.

How long will the sun shine?

It's hard to imagine a time when the sun no longer shines. All life on earth depends on the heat, light and other kinds of energy given off by the sun. Will there ever be a day when the sun stops shining?

Scientists predict that the sun could shine for about 10 billion

What lives on the moon?

The moon is about one quarter the size of Earth. It measures 2160 miles in diameter. But the rock that makes up the moon is not as dense as our rock, so Earth is eighty-one times heavier than the moon.

This means that the gravity of the moon is different. Gravity determines how heavy something is, and the gravity on the moon is only one-sixth that of Earth's. If everything is only one-sixth as heavy, this means that you could jump very high on the moon or fall a long way without hurting yourself. And there are other consequences of having a low gravity. Earth's gravity is strong enough to hold around us a layer of light air that forms our atmosphere. But the moon has no air at all. Because there is no air, there is no water. And without air and water, of course, nothing could live on the moon.

years. The sun is already about 4 600 000 000 years old, so it will probably shine for at least another 5 000 000 000 years.

When the sun does change about 5 000 000 000 years from now, it will probably first become so hot that the earth's temperature will be too high for life to exist on it. Then the sun will lose most of its energy and become dark and cold.

DID YOU KNOW . . . the moon is 384 000 kilometres (240 000 miles) away from the earth.

Where was the biggest volcanic eruption?

Volcanoes have always fascinated and terrified people. Legends say they are the doorways to hell and the houses of fire gods.

The worst volcanic explosion we know of happened at Krakatoa in Indonesia in 1883, when the volcano on this tiny island exploded four times in one day!

Much of the island was blown into tiny pieces. The third explosion was so loud it was heard from as far as 4800 kilometres (3000 miles) away. Dust and giant pieces of rock shot 80 kilometres (50 miles) into the air and tons of red-hot lava showered down on the island. The explosion was so powerful that the top of the volcano toppled over and sank into the sea. This caused fierce waves as high as 37 metres (120 feet) that crashed across nearby islands and killed 36 000 people.

It took three months for all of the volcanic ash to fall back down to earth. The burnt ash floated in the air, sometimes making the day as dark as night. Other days it made the sun look green and the moon look blue! It was the most powerful explosion we have ever seen and caused one of the worst disasters we have ever known.

DID YOU KNOW . . . the biggest geyser ever to erupt was Waimango geyser in New Zealand, which in 1904 sent up a column of steaming water over 500 metres (1500 feet) high!

Where do diamonds come from?

All over the world, diamonds are symbols of beauty and wealth.

But did you know that each of these precious stones was made millions of years ago in a volcano? To begin with, the rock in the volcano was under enormous pressure and very high temperatures. Then gradually, over millions of years, it cooled down. If there was carbon in the rock, the temperature and pressure forced the carbon to form crystals as it cooled down.

As time passed, the hardened volcanic rock gradually washed into streams or was blown away by the wind. So miners search for diamonds on top of and around old volcanoes.

What are geysers?

Geysers are a special kind of hot spring. They look like fountains when they spurt hot water and steam into the air.

You can see geysers in areas where a volcano has erupted within the last million years. In these places, there is lots of hot rock not far below the earth's surface. In order for a geyser to form, there must be passageways reaching from the surface to the hot rock. Water drains into the passageways and some touches the rock. This water is heated until it boils.

Steam from the boiling water takes up more space than the water, so it pushes the water up and out of the passageway.

Most of the water drains back into the geyser and the heating starts again. Some geysers erupt every few minutes, while others can be seen only every few years.

ARE YOU GUYS SURE THERE'S UNDER-GROUND WATER DOWN THERE?

YOU'LL SEE IN A FEW MORE SECONDS!

What is a UFO?

If you have ever seen something in the sky and didn't know what it was, then you may have seen an unidentified flying object, or UFO. In 1947, a Chicago businessman was the first person in modern times to report a UFO. Since then, thousands of people have seen them.

In 1952, the United States government organized a panel of scientists to study UFOs and try and figure out what they were. Most of the time, the sightings turned out to be bright planets, meteors, clouds, airplanes, birds, balloons, searchlights, optical illusions or someone's imagination. Some people have even tried to make up evidence of UFO sightings, like the man who photographed upside-down soup plates hovering over a vacuum cleaner hose and claimed they were flying saucers.

But a small number of UFO sightings are still a mystery. A few scientists and many other people believe that some of the UFOs have been visitors from outer space. Most scientists believe that there is no such thing. What do *you* think?

How many planets are there?

Nine planets circle around our sun. Earth is one of them, the third one out from the sun.

Closest to the sun, Mercury is small and hot, with no air around it. Next is Venus, which we see as the first and brightest star at night. Venus is the same size as Earth, but on Venus the sky rains sulphuric acid onto a burning hot surface. After Earth is Mars, which has a thin atmosphere. It is possible that life exists on Mars though no one knows for sure.

Beyond Mars are four giant planets, and tiny frozen Pluto. The giant planets—Jupiter, Saturn, Uranus and Neptune— are all much larger than Earth. Jupiter and Saturn may be only huge balls of liquid gas and dust. It is now thought that most of these giant planets are surrounded by rings, but it is the rings of Saturn that can be seen with a telescope from Earth.

Some of the planets have little planets circling around them. We have our moon, Jupiter has thirteen, and one of Saturn's moons is as big as the planet Mercury!

Why are there waves?

If you've ever thrown a rock into a pond you know that ripples spread out from the spot where the rock went in. These are actually little waves.

Lakes and oceans have big waves that are caused in much the same way. Often it's wind that starts a wave in the ocean. But waves are not caused by wind alone. What happens is that after the wind pushes the water up, gravity—the force that holds us down on the ground—pulls the water back down. The water goes so far down that the force of the water underneath bounces it back up again, making a wave.

The wave moves across the water, but the water under the wave doesn't move very much. This is why waves bob things on the water up and down, but don't carry them very far.

Is the earth flat?

Look out your window. Does the earth appear to curve? Probably not. It looks flat to you just as it did to early explorers.

Some people even believed that a giant named Atlas supported the earth on his shoulders, while others believed a huge turtle carried it around on its back.

It wasn't until the fifteenth century that astronomers and explorers began to realize that the earth was round. They noticed that distant sailing ships disappeared from the bottom

DID YOU KNOW . . . if the earth's yearly rainfall fell at once, the world would be buried under a metre (3 feet) of water!

up, as if they were going around a curve. The only reasonable explanation was that the earth must be round. We take it for granted, but those early explorers really had to have a lot of courage to test their ideas.

Today we know that the earth is not perfectly round. It is slightly flattened at the North and South poles, which makes it an oval shape.

Where is the world's largest waterfall?

The waterfall with the greatest amount of water flowing over it is in Zaire in central Africa. The Boyoma Falls is actually a series of seven cataracts that stretch along 100 kilometres (60 miles) of the Lualaba River. The water drops 60 metres (200 feet) over that distance. Every *second,* 17 000 cubic metres (600 000 cubic feet) of water pass any one point on the falls.

DID YOU KNOW . . . the highest waterfall in the world is on Devil's Mountain in Venezuela. Angel Falls drops 963 metres (3213 feet) into the Carrao River.

How deep is the ocean?

Very, very deep. Far down in the ocean depths, the water is very cold and it is darker than midnight. But creatures live at those depths—it seems that there is life in the ocean all the way to the bottom.

There are three main depths to the ocean bottom. Close to shore, there are continental shelves, where the bottom is only about a hundred metres (300 feet) under water. Then the shelf drops off to the true ocean bottom, which lies at an average depth of 4000 metres (13 000 feet). The Pacific Ocean is a little deeper than the Atlantic.

Then, deepest of all, are the trenches. These are valleys on the ocean bottom, where the crust of the earth is pulled open. One of these is the Marianas Trench in the western Pacific. Here is the Challenger Deep, the deepest place in all the oceans—it is almost 11 kilometres (7 miles) below sea level!

DID YOU KNOW . . . ship captains use "tide tables" to tell them when to come into a harbor, just as bus passengers use timetables to tell them when a bus is coming. But tide tables are more dependable—tide times never change their regular pattern!

Where are the highest tides in the world?

Did you think that the world's highest tides must be in a tropical place like Hawaii? If you did, you're wrong: the highest tides in the world are found in Canada.

In the Bay of Fundy, which is between New Brunswick and Nova Scotia, the tides can rise and fall as much as 18 metres (60 feet). In most other places, tides usually rise by only about 2 metres (6 feet).

The reason for the giant tides is the unusual shape, size and depth of the bay, which combine to increase the effects of the tidal water flowing into the bay from the Atlantic Ocean.

So if you're ever standing on the beach in the Bay of Fundy and someone yells "the tide's coming in," you'd better move a long way back if you don't want to get a soaker!

How many oceans are there?

If you look at a globe, you'll see that the surface of the earth is covered in one huge ocean with big islands here and there. We call these big islands continents.

Looking at it another way, there are three main oceans which together cover more than 70 percent of the earth's surface. The three oceans are the Pacific, the Atlantic and the Indian.

The Pacific is the largest and deepest and covers more than one third of our planet. It lies between the Americas and China.

The Atlantic is the second largest and it lies between the Americas and Europe.

The Indian Ocean lies between Africa and Australia.

At the earth's poles are two frozen oceans called the Arctic and the Antarctic. Some people think of them as oceans in their own right, while others think they're just parts of the main three. They say that the Arctic is the northernmost part of the Atlantic, and that the Antarctic is formed where the Atlantic, Pacific and Indian oceans meet at the South Pole.

What causes earthquakes?

Have you ever felt the earth shake? Your answer will depend on where you live. If you live in Alaska, California or Mexico, you might very well say yes.

Earthquakes are caused by movements of the earth. The outer 30 to 50 kilometres (20 to 30 miles) of our planet forms a hard rock crust, which is floating on a sea of molten rock. The crust is separated into about 20 huge pieces, or plates, and the lines where the plates join each other are called faults. At the faults, the earth's crust is weak, and it is here that earthquakes are likely to happen.

Forces inside the earth are always pushing the plates against each other. When the force becomes too great, the pressure is released at a fault line. The earth bends, the ground trembles, the crust breaks—and it's an earthquake!

To understand what a big earthquake feels like, imagine standing on the deck of a ship during rough weather. The ground beneath your feet would roll and shake, and you might even lose your balance. A really powerful earthquake can knock down an entire city!

But don't fear, even though there are about 100 earthquakes a month, most of them are so mild that they don't do any damage.

What is quicksand?

You have probably seen people trapped in quicksand in movies, their bodies slowly vanishing into the muck and their hat floating on the surface. But quicksand is not nearly as dangerous as movies lead us to believe. In fact, people are not sucked into quicksand but some people do panic and then drown in it.

For quicksand to form, you need a hole in the ground filled with sand or mud. Then you need water flowing upward from the bottom of the hole, such as a stream emerging from underground. Imagine a very thick soup made out of water and sand and you have the picture.

Since quicksand is much heavier than water, you can float on it higher than you can on water. So if you feel yourself sinking in a mud soup, don't panic. Simply lie down and slowly roll yourself to solid ground.

What is the shape of a falling raindrop?

Draw what you think a raindrop looks like.

You probably drew a tear-drop shape, because that's how raindrops are usually drawn in cartoons. That idea comes from the way a water droplet stretches itself before falling off something. But once the droplet starts falling, it becomes round. Raindrops are always perfectly round, like millions of tiny balls falling from the sky.

Why do we talk about it raining "cats and dogs"?

Have you ever been walking outside when it was raining so hard that you felt the sky was about to fall? If you have, then you've been out when it was raining cats and dogs.

Although no one has ever seen it rain cats and dogs there have been reports of it raining both rocks and fish. Experts believe that tornadoes may have picked up the objects in one spot and then, after the winds had died down, dropped them in another.

As for "raining cats and dogs," the expression has been used for hundreds of years. It may relate to Norse mythology that associates the dog with the wind and the cat with storms.

Next time you're out, and it's raining cats and dogs, try to avoid stepping in any poodles.

Why is the sky blue?

Two things work together to make the sky blue: sunlight and dust particles in the earth's atmosphere.

It may look as if sunlight has no color, but in fact it is made up of all the colors of the rainbow. Try holding a prism in the sunlight. You'll see that the light breaks up into red, orange, yellow, green, blue, indigo and violet. This is similar to what happens to the sun's rays when they reach the earth's atmosphere. They are broken up into all these colors by billions of tiny dust and water particles there.

The red, orange and yellow rays can travel through the atmosphere and continue down to earth. However, it is not so easy for the green, violet and indigo rays to get through. The blue rays are stopped altogether. They are reflected by the particles in the atmosphere. Since it is the blue rays that stay up in the sky, we can look up and see a brilliant blue on a sunny day.

What are "all the colors of the rainbow"?

There are seven colors in every rainbow. The colors blend into each other, which is why people usually see only four or five colors. The seven colors in each rainbow are: violet, indigo (a deep violet-blue), blue, green, yellow, orange, and red. The amount of space each color takes up varies from rainbow to rainbow, depending mainly on the size of the raindrops in which the rainbow forms.

What is a glacier?

Glaciers are great moving blankets of ice. They begin as snow in high mountains and near the North Pole and the South Pole. In these places, the weather does not get warm enough to melt all the snow in the spring. Each year new snow piles on top of old snow and gradually the large amounts of snow freeze.

Tiny ice crystals in the snow join together to form a special type of ice. This ice is unusual because it is extremely hard, and it has the ability to flow. The ice at the bottom is plastic-like because of the great weight above it. This makes it possible for the whole mass of ice to slide slowly along the ground. It's a little like what would happen if you pressed down on a ball of dough. The dough would start to push outward.

When the mass of ice starts to flow, it is called a glacier. Glaciers are extremely powerful. They can move rocks, trees and anything else that gets in their way. If you travel through the mountains in the western part of Canada or the United States, you will likely see some glaciers.

Where is the least populated place on earth?

Do you want to be alone? If you do, Antarctica would be a good place to visit. It has an area of over 14 million square kilometres (5.5 million square miles), but only a few thousand people live there. And that's during the summer. Only a few hundred stay for the bitterly cold winter. Just about all the residents are scientists who live there

Is Greenland really green?

When you hear the name Greenland, it's logical to imagine a place covered with thick grass, flowing streams and miles of green forests. But this is not what Greenland looks like.

Greenland is the largest island in the world. An enormous glacier covers 85 percent of the island and is 3000 metres (10 000 feet) thick in some places. Most of Greenland is really white!

It was called Greenland by Eric the Red who sailed there from Iceland in the year 982. Eric the Red wanted settlers to come to the land he had discovered, so he called it Greenland to emphasize how beautiful it was. At that time, Greenland actually was warm enough to grow crops and raise livestock. But after the year 1200, the weather became colder and by 1400, there were no farming settlements left. Greenland is one of the *least* green countries in the world.

DID YOU KNOW . . . thousands of years ago, glaciers covered almost a third of the land in the world.

because of their job, not because they want to.

At Vostok, a Soviet research station, the average temperature for the warmest month is –33° C (–27° F). Temperatures are much warmer on the coast, but still well below freezing. You can see why not many people want to live there.

Index